THE PROCESSED WOMAN

Your Purpose Is On The Other Side!

Dr. Shaurice E. Mullins, PhD, CHLC

Copyright © 2013 Dr. Shaurice E. Mullins, Phd, Chlc

All rights reserved

ISBN: 0615862039

ISBN 13: 9780615862033

Library of Congress Control Number: 2013914866
The Processed Woman, Inc., Wilson, NC

Dedication

To my children:
Bryan, Jamee', Roderick, Joshua, Rianah
and my beautiful granddaughter Janiyah. I love
you dearly.

Acknowledgements

Where does one start to thank those that joined you, walked beside you, and helped you along the way continuously? I can never thank those enough who urged me to publish my writings, to take the thoughts and the things I had already written down on paper and share them with the world. Those who I have met along the way who encouraged me, inspired me, and uplifted me in ways that words could never express. So at last, here it is. So, perhaps this book and its pages will be seen as a "thank you" to the thousands of you who have helped make my life what is today. Much of what I have learned over the years came as the result of being a mother of five and a grandmother. To my five wonderful children: Bryan, Jamee', Roderick, Joshua, Rianah, and my granddaughter Janiyah, who has inspired and encouraged me in their own ways. Life would not be the same without any of you. The six of you are my inspiration…Thank You! I also have to thank Sharlene Wall for taking this journey with me for many years and whose love and dedication over the years has encouraged, motivated, and inspired me. Your love and kindness is definitely God sent. Thank you for being a true sister. I also need to thank Blondell Biggs-Davis, a wonderful woman whose love, kindness, and belief in me changed my life completely. Thank you for being a sister, spiritual mother, and friend. Words cannot express my gratitude to Team Processed Woman, Present Truth Holistic Ministries, and Finding My Way Fellowship Center for their love and support. This would not have been possible without you. To William Raymond and Jamisha Raymond: thank you for your dedication, love, and support. It is truly a blessing to have you both in my life. I also have to thank Robert Jackson for his patience, love, friendship, and support. I love you more than you will ever know. Finally, I am forever indebted to my parents, brother, family members, and friends for their understanding, endless patience, and encouragement when it was needed most.

Contents

The Processed Woman 1

The Processed Woman Knows
   How to Establish and Maintain
   a Positive Attitude 7

Ten Kingdom Keys to Maintaining
   a Positive Attitude 9

The Processed Woman Has the
   Mentality of an Overcomer 13

Ten Kingdom Things to Know
   in Order to Overcome: 17

The Processed Woman Understands
   and Controls Her Emotions 21

Understanding the Emotional Process 23

The Processed Woman Seeks the Path of Bliss 25

Pleasure Seeking vs. Bliss 27

The Processed Woman Knows How
   to Remain in Perfect Peace 33

The Processed Woman is Skilled at
   Using What She's Got to Get
   What She Wants...37

The Processed Woman Desires to
   Live a Life of Integrity.......................................41

The Processed Woman Knows
   She Must Overcome the
   Fear of Failure...45

The Processed Woman Understands
   the Importance of Forgiveness 51

The Processed Woman Walks in
   Her Destiny and Fulfills Her Purpose 57

The Processed Woman

Process

A *process* is defined as a natural phenomenon marked by gradual changes leading toward a particular result. In other words, the circumstances or challenges we face in life are all part of the *process* of our development. Every challenge we face in life leads to our soul's evolution and will ultimately push us toward our God-given purpose.

We know that God has an expected end for each of us. God told Jeremiah, "Before I formed thee in the belly, I knew thee; and before thou came forth out of the womb I sanctified thee, and I ordained thee a prophet unto the nations" (Jeremiah 1:5).[1] Just as God told Jeremiah, we, too, are each called,

---

[1] This book employs the Authorized (King James) Version of the Bible

ordained, and sanctified for a purpose. These plans are laid even before we are born. Yes, God has a plan designed with *you* in mind! Unfortunately, we often spend the majority of our time trying to master an imitation of someone else. We must learn to be ourselves-the individuals God created us to be.

As we each strive to become the person God intended, we will discover our hidden potential.

God never intends for us to fail. Neither would he allow us to stray into death before our time. Rather, the incidents we encounter on this journey we call life, were designed to strengthen us. God clearly states in Luke 17:21, that "the kingdom of God is within". Here, God reveals that he resides with us.

We are vessels that hold a certain ever-present power, and this power is God. If you walk to the ocean and fill a glass with water, the ocean water may be displaced-but it remains ocean water nonetheless. Our bodies are the containers of something awesome, powerful, and magnificent!

Another important biblical passage states, "Greater is He that is in me than he that is in the world" (1 John 4:4). Do we really understand what this statement means? If we truly understood this passage, we would know that nothing exists outside of us that is greater than the power residing inside us. This power ignites confidence in the face of opposition. It ensures that whatever affliction or obstacle we may face, negativity must bow down to the greater power within us.

Jesus states in John 10:10, "I am come that they might have life, and they might have it more abundantly." The abundance he mentions isn't simply financial. Jesus died that we might walk in our God-given authority. Upon his death, we became joint-heirs to this authority. This gave us access to the same power he accessed. Jesus died that we may have access to the keys to the Kingdom within. In Matthew 16:19, Jesus states, "And I will give unto thee the keys of the kingdom of heaven..." His sacrifice has given you, as a believer, certain birth rights-but you must utilize these keys to unlock your individual potential and power.

Every challenge we face processes us for purpose! Processes us to make us stronger! Processes us to give us the wisdom and insight to maneuver through our very own "Soul-Evolving Process".

> With each "Soul-Evolving Process" we gain enlightenment and awareness of our purpose in life.

We cease to whine and complain, and we instead realize our foundation is sure. We know in whom to trust. As Romans 8:28 states, "And we know that all things work together for good to them that love

God, to them who are the called according to his purpose." The word "all" in that statement demonstrates that good *and* bad things will work together for our good!

Purpose

A *purpose* is defined as the reason something exists, is done, or is made. Each of us has a "Soul Purpose." This purpose gives us something to offer the world. Many people know very little about their Soul Purpose. This leads to confusion or misinformation about the *purpose* of the *process*. It is necessary to go through the process to get to the purpose. Many people are unfulfilled in life because they are uncertain of their goals or failing to accomplish their goals. They perform various tasks day in and day out, but they are not living the lives they were intended to live.

> Your Soul Purpose will be discovered when your talents, passions and qualities work together to form the most magnificent version of you.

This perfected version will be unveiled upon the successful completion of your "process."

When these qualities are intentionally and "purposely" acknowledged, used, and cultivated, they coalesce into a specific goal that can be offered back as a service to humanity. Although many of these qualities may be hidden, they already exist within you.

You do not have to look beyond yourself for these God-given talents. They may lie dormant, but God gave them to you expecting you to utilizing them (Matthew 25:14-30).

In order to experience greater joy, health and wealth, you must know your "Soul Purpose." Once your purpose has been discovered, true fulfillment is found. This is a sign of an accomplished life. When a person is truly fulfilled they have found their place in life and contentment with themselves. It will take dedication, but you will experience prosperity in every area of your life once you have successfully sought and carefully attended to your gifts and purpose.

A *Processed Woman* has certain qualities that we will cover in the following chapters. "See, I have tested you in the furnace of affliction" states Isaiah 48:10. A furnace is hot and uncomfortable. Like a clay vase in a kiln, a Processed Woman has been refined through life's experiences. A furnace typically is hot and definitely uncomfortable. Life can be uncomfortable and extremely painful to bear-but as a Processed Woman thrives, she experiences praise, glory and honor as God reveals himself through her life.

The Processed Woman Knows How to Establish and Maintain a Positive Attitude

We may subconsciously speak a lot of words that often can lead to vain babblings. Your true feelings and beliefs are reflected in your attitude. "As a man thinketh in his heart, so is he" (Proverbs 23:7). What you truly believe about yourself and your life is reflected in your daily attitude. Establishing and maintaining a positive attitude in challenging situations will lead to wisdom and spiritual power.

A positive attitude comes from seeing things as they really are. This *"seeing"* is an inner understanding of one's life and being.

Never label life's challenges as ultimately detrimental. We should learn to care very little about the things in life that we can't avoid. What is the point of allowing these things to zap us of our positive attitude, strength, and power?

We have the power to overcome any Soul-Evolving Challenge; to do so, we must simply establish and maintain a positive attitude. Our attitude triggers internal and external responses. External responses are those from people around us; in other words, their negative and positive responses toward us. Internal responses come from the subconscious mind. The subconscious processes positive and negative habits and thoughts. A negative attitude damages you psychologically, physically and spiritually.

To draw out positive responses and create a better life, you should strive to maintain a positive attitude. Remember, your attitude reflects what you *really* believe!

Ten Kingdom Keys to Maintaining a Positive Attitude

KEY #1 – Do not dwell on past mistakes. Doing so damages you psychologically by accepting thoughts of failure into your thought patterns.

KEY #2 – What you think about yourself and your life is accepted as true (Proverbs 23:7). This is very important because thoughts are *things*, and can manifest beyond your mind. What you think about long enough will become your reality.

KEY #3 – Negative thoughts can cause physical damage. Negative thoughts will manifest in the body in the form of illness and disease. It has been said that we should "speak" life. I believe we should *think* life as well.

THE PROCESSED WOMAN

KEY #4 – No matter how bleak the outlook, God will show you the way. According to Psalms 37:23, your steps are ordered.

KEY #5 – It is imperative to practice prayer and meditation. Daily acts of prayer and thanksgiving enforce a positive outlook. Wisdom attained through prayer assists us in gaining the insight to raise us above any problem.

KEY #6 – Your life has purpose. Your life has meaning, and you are being directed by God to fulfill your purpose. In spite of what it looks like, victory is your name!

KEY #7 – You are already healed. In the case of ill health and disease, the price has been paid. Jesus paid the price for your healing. The spiritual nature within you has the power over every negative thought and disease. Jesus sacrificed to let us experience healing (Isaiah 53:5).

KEY #8 – Current circumstances are temporary. Learn to speak life. No obstacle can stand in the presence of the spoken Word of God. In the midst of a seemingly dead situation, speak life! Stand on the truth found in God's Word. Believe what the Word says about you and temporary negativity will soon disappear.

KEY #9 – Denounce the lies and believe the truth. If you are experiencing temporary financial lack, know that God will lead you to sustenance. God wants you to prosper both physically and financially. You may not be where you desire to be financially, but the truth is in God. The power to break the bonds of lack rests in you, for God rests in you.

KEY #10 – Accept Responsibility. When negative events occur in your life, spend less time blaming others and more time seeking God. Seek God for wisdom in every situation. Do not get stuck in the "If only I hadn't..." mentality. Know that no situation has the power to disturb you, move you, or defeat you unless you allow it. What has passed has passed. Accept responsibility where responsibility is due, and take the necessary steps to turn it around.

All experiences, no matter how trying, come to you as a lesson. You will acquire wisdom, and power through the lesson. Walk in confidence and keep a positive attitude, knowing that all things are working together for your good!

Remember the lesson from 2 Corinthians 4:16-18: "For which cause we faint not; but though our outward man perish, yet the inward man is renewed day by day. For our light affliction which is but for a moment, worketh for us a far more exceeding and eternal weight of glory. While we look not at the things which are seen, but at the things which are not seen; for the things which are seen are temporal; but the things which are not seen are eternal."

The Processed Woman Has the Mentality of an Overcomer

With every experience comes an anointing or power to endure and overcome.

So says Revelations 4:1: "Thou are worthy, O Lord, to receive glory and honour and power: for thou hast created all things and for thy pleasure they are and were created." With this knowledge, we must bless the Lord at all times! Negative situations have not come to destroy you. Instead, they come to make you! Every soul must grow and evolve. We may seem to lack the strength to make it through the toughest challenges in life. At times, we may even feel as if we will die before the negativity relents. Remember, though, that it is by these things God shall get the glory! In these times, we must be like Job. "Although he slay me," we must say, "yet will I trust him" (Job 13:15).

Confidence and Trust

Confidence is defined as the belief, trust, worthiness or reliability in a person or thing. It includes full trust and reliance. To have and maintain the mentality of an overcomeer there must not only be confidence in God, but also trust. *Trust* is complete certainty of future payment for goods received. It is confident expectation. When you have confidence in God, you receive insight in every situation. Although hell may break lose all around you, the spirit of confusion leaves and you find yourself at peace.

God did not give us the spirit of fear. (2 Timothy 1:7) Fear is a killer of confidence. Fear leaves us hopeless and powerless. But there will come a time in our lives where we are no longer walking by faith; we will walk instead in "knowing"! The knowing will be one of our God. It will be the knowledge that you can safely rely on the Word of God. You will transition from hoping he will work it out to knowing it has already been worked out. It's already done!

"But thou art holy, O thou inhabit the praises of Israel. Our fathers trusted in thee: they cried unto thee *and were delivered*: they trusted thee, and were not confounded. (Psalms 22:3-5). All of God is available to every person. Nothing is ever withheld from a sincere seeker of the truth.

Ephesians 3:20 tells us "Now to him that is able to do exceeding abundantly above all we ask or think *according to the power that worketh in us*. Where there is fear, there is no confidence and there is no power!

> Your power is locked and tangled up with your confidence. No man can do anything unless he has the confidence to know he can achieve it.

Overcoming is the acceptance that God is at the highest order of things. If you truly know this, your actions will follow your acceptance. There is no need of crying all night if your confidence is in God. There is no need for sleepless nights if you know that God neither slumbers nor sleeps. Somebody needs to sleep...*You!*

But how much do we really strive to overcome? Do we have the confidence to know that we can in the first place? If your attempts to overcome life challenges have been difficult, something *must* change. The change must take place within you. To overcome outwardly, you must first overcome inwardly!

Ten Kingdom Things to Know in Order to Overcome:

Know that:

KEY #1 – The power to overcome is within you. The only thing that needs to change is your perception of yourself. God is in you, thus you have everything needed to have, do, or be anything you desire. All else is an illusion.

KEY #2 – Greater is he that is in you than he that is in the world.

Know that there is nothing outside of you greater than the God within you.

KEY #3 – You have your own identity. Because of Christ, we each have access to the Father. There is no one greater than you. God looks at us all in the same way. Although each of us has been given different assignments, duties, and functions in the kingdom, no one is better or greater than the other. God has no respect of person!

KEY #4 – Know that you have a "personal assignment" while on the earth. No one can fulfill your purpose but you. Your assignment and talents were given to you before you were born (Jeremiah 1:5). Your destiny and purpose was also preordained and locked within you before your birth. All things that will ever be in your life are within you. All you have to do is seek God and he will give you the knowledge to open every door to your destiny!

KEY #5 – There is purpose in your pain. Know that your steps have been ordered. All things you will ever do, every mistake, every evil deed, God knew of and yet he still chose you! Each of your actions, good or bad is for your growth. With this in mind, know also that every decision we make, leads to a consequence. It is up to you to choose. Just as the indicator light comes on when the fuel is low in your car, every negative thing in your life is an indicator that you need to do something different. Redirect your course!

KEY #6 – You deserve the best. Do not buy into the illusion that God desires you to suffer. You are his child, why would He desire you to suffer? Parents do not wish to see their children suffer. Life and Death are set before you. Choose life. No man should think temptation and suffering are the will of God. Most negative things are brought upon us by following the desires of the flesh. God has a divine plan. He wishes us well. God does not seek to punish you. You were created for his glory!

KEY #7 – You must have confidence. Have confidence in God and confidence in yourself. The power to defeat, cast down and overcome anything is within you!

KEY #8 – You may be an outcast, but you are never forgotten. An outcast is a person who has been rejected or cast out. Many of us have been rejected for most of our lives. You may have been talked about, misunderstood, or ostracized. You may have been told that you would never amount to anything. You may be a social outcast. As a matter of fact, you may have even given up on yourself. There may not seem to be a way to turn things around. But it is not over until God says it's over! Micah 7:7-8 states, "Therefore I will look unto the Lord; I will wait for the God of my salvation: my God will hear me. Rejoice not against me, O mine enemy: when I fall, I shall arise; when I sit in darkness, the Lord shall be a light unto me."

KEY #9– God's got your back! Know that in your weakest moments, the strength of the Lord is made perfect (II Corinthians 12:19). With every day that passes, your inner strength will increase to endure through your circumstances. You shall come out stronger than ever! If God is for you, who can be against you? No one or nothing! Psalm 145:14 states, "The Lord upholdeth all that fall, and raiseth up all those that be bowed down."

KEY #10 – You must stand on the Word of God. In spite of appearances, know that God watches over his Word (Jeremiah 1:12). There is a creative power in the Word of God. Use it and you will overcome any obstacle in your way! You are not a victim; you are an overcomeer!

The Processed Woman Understands and Controls Her Emotions

Having emotions is not a bad thing. As a matter of fact, too many people discuss emotions in a very negative manner. The key is to acknowledge our feelings and deal with them. By doing so, we learn to control our emotions rather than letting them control us. Emotions are very powerful. They serve as sensors or messengers to tell us what is going on around us and in us. Suppressing our emotions or trying to mask them with affirmations will not work. These energies, whether they represent depression, anger, fear, grief, joy or love must be addressed and explored in order to experience the freedom we wish to have in our lives.

So what are emotions? The word itself says a lot if we would simply pay attention to it. *E-motions*.

Motion is defined as the act or process of moving. These things we call emotions are *"energy in motion."* They are not always in us, as they are constantly moving *around* us as well.

Have you ever been in a great mood and walked into a room with an upset person? Suddenly you "feel" upset or angry as well. Emotions have the ability to act upon us and elicit a physical response. That is why being emotionally overwhelmed often leads to headaches, chest pains, and other physical ailments.

We say our "feelings" are hurt, leading to anger and tears. In truth, your feelings are
not hurt: your body is. It has become overloaded with emotions you have not learned to handle.

For many years traditional science -medicine as well as psychology- defined our emotions as chemical reactions and extensions of thought. To control emotions, you must monitor and change your thought patterns. This is a matter of choice. *Thought* is knowledge based on memory. Thought patterns are merely memories engraved in your brain patterns.

> Once you change a thought pattern, you can control the emotion linked to past actions.

Once the emotion is acknowledged it can be dealt with. This frees you to go forward in the *now*.

Understanding the Emotional Process

When you encounter challenges, several things take place. First of all, an emotion acts upon you. It may be anger, jealousy, sadness, loneliness, or any other emotion triggered by the circumstances. Next, the thought enters your mind and sends a corresponding signal to the brain. Your brain processes the emotion acting upon you, causing you to say "I am angry."

To the untrained mind, these things happen too fast to recognize the steps within the process. With careful attention, however, you will be able to monitor this process. I call the next step the "bulldozer effect." During this phase, the body is flooded with emotions so quickly and thoroughly, it becomes overwhelmed. These emotions "bulldoze" in so destructively, they sometimes cause a total emotional breakdown. These emotions then move through the physical body, spiritual body, and soul of a person.

The soul is the "*seat*" of our emotions. It is the resting place for all emotions to come and "*sit*" within us. These emotions, whether good or bad, will sit in your soul until they are acknowledged and dealt with. God can divide the spirit and soul, and through this separation the spirit works within us to master every emotional pain in our lives. Hebrews 4:12 states, "For the Word of God is quick, and powerful, and sharper than any two edged sword, piercing even to the dividing asunder of soul and spirit, and of the joints and marrow, and is a discerner of the thoughts and intents of the heart."

> Only when the spirit and the soul are divided by the Word of Truth can the soul become subject to the spirit.

People remain bound by their emotions when they fail to acknowledge them. This step can neither be skipped nor ignored. You cannot deny your felt emotions. It is not wrong to have emotions. I merely suggest that we need to understand emotions and their calibration. By doing so, we learn to apply our knowledge to control our emotions, stopping them from becoming bulldozers in our lives.

The Processed Woman Seeks the Path of Bliss

Love is one of the most desired emotions. It is also one of the most misunderstood. The word is used so loosely these days, it holds very little weight in the minds and hearts of humankind. When hearing the word "love" from another human being, some wonder whether the emotion is genuine or false. Do you really know what love is?

Love is sacrificial and cannot be measured by the pleasure-seeking tendencies of humans. Love is unconditional and is not based on the performance or personality of another individual. Love is God. Because of this, love is patient, kind, merciful and true. It does not turn off and on like a light switch. Love sees greatness and potential in people. It isn't judgmental. Instead, it causes you to be quick to restore, uphold and offer yourself in ways that might seem unnatural to those who have no idea what love really is.

Love seeks peace. It does this in spite of what another person may or may not do. Love is quick to see God-the greatness-in another person. It does not seek pleasure and is not selfish. Pleasure seeking, after all, is one of the main reasons people never experience real love.

Pleasure Seeking vs. Bliss

The Budda said, *"There is pleasure and there is bliss. Forgo the first to possess the second."* We must learn to mature from our pleasure-seeking tendencies if we are ever to enjoy what true love is. Only through true love can we experience bliss. Pleasure is temporal, but bliss is eternal. Bliss is inward and pleasure is outward.

This brings me back to my foundational question: Do we really know what love is? Pleasure-seeking causes us to seek out things simply because they are new. Once the newness is gone, we find ourselves desiring pleasure in something else. For example, a man might say he is in love with a woman. He claims that she is all he desires and that he cannot live without her. He pursues her until she is overwhelmed by his passion. He tells her that he adores her and that he wants no one else in the world. He wines and dines her. Ultimately, sex enters the relationship. Soon after having sex with the woman, the man loses interest in the very person he claimed he couldn't live without. He moves on to the next conquest.

> When we do not know the difference between love and pleasure seeking, we take risks as women.

The woman mentioned above is left devastated. Truly, she too was seeking pleasure; she became wrapped up in the man's words instead of seeing him for his desperate self. A man cannot give what is not in him to give. If he can only offer pleasure-seeking, then pleasure seeking is all he will give and ever have-at least until he realizes what he is actually doing. In the end, the search for pleasure always leads to misery.

How can we truly love or know when we do not love ourselves enough to discover our Soul Purpose? We constantly seek things beyond ourselves, and these things are the same temporary pleasures leading to our demise.

> Loving someone is only a temporary illusion if you do not love yourself.

It is also an illusion if you have not discovered the bliss within yourself. Simply put, that artificial substitute is no match for real love.

Unfortunately, many people will live their entire lives and never find bliss. They will never discover their true selves because they are too afraid to let go of the temporal things and seek true bliss. Pleasure and happiness are nearly identical and ruthlessly sought after.

Seeking happiness beyond yourself, however, will not lead to validation.

We seek happiness, yet we tend to think that finding the "perfect" man will make us happy. This is not true happiness or joy, merely another crutch. Being with someone else will not solve your problems-if anything, it will only intensify them. Happiness is a form of pleasure that comes and goes like the wind.

Happiness is superficial if you are only happy when the man you "love" acts the way you want him to. Accepting this type of happiness will leave you feeling like a car on a rollercoaster. This is why finding inner peace is so necessary.

Joy, unlike happiness, does not come from anything beyond the self. This inner joy fills us in spite of what is going on around us; this is what gives us peace. As the scriptures tells us, "... the joy of the Lord is your strength" (Nehemiah 8:10).

Joy is not based on anything around you. It is a state of inner peace beyond any situation or circumstance. "And the peace of God, which passeth all understanding shall keep your hearts and minds through Christ Jesus" (Philippians 4:7). When all hell is breaking loose around you, and yet you are not moved, then you have reached a place of joy in your life.

But is there truly a place even beyond joy? Indeed there is! It is *bliss*, a state the "Processed Woman" seeks to obtain and maintain. This state of *bliss*, or unspeakable joy can only be obtained when we stop looking outside for affirmation and learn to instead look within. Look within and know that what we seek is there already.

> *Bliss* is not materialistic. It is not a person, place or thing. It is a state of mind. It is a consciousness, and this can only be obtained by the embodiment of the *truth* of oneself.

This truth reveals that God can be found within you in his entirety. It reveals that within you is the power to have, to be, or to do whatever you desire. Worry ceases when you realize you are a co-creator and that things around you will change when you truly "*see*" the change.

Until we can reach bliss in our lives, we will never have the love or peace we truly desire. We will continue to live in a dog-eat-dog world. In this world people chase after love, other people, and things yet those things-and yet those things being chased seem to run away, forever unable to be caught.

A woman ceases to compete for anything when she adopts a bliss consciousness. Her pleasure-seeking tendencies disappear, and she finds peace. She knows what is for *her* will come to *her*.

Seeking pleasure only leads to misery and pain over and over again. Get rid of your pleasure-seeking tendencies and go within. Get to know yourself and all the greatness within. Consider 2 Corinthians 4:7: "But we have this treasure in earthen vessels, that the excellency of the power may be of God, and not of us." There is a treasure in your earthen vessel, and it is the the kingdom. Seek this kingdom, and all the things you desire will be given to you!

The Processed Woman Knows How to Remain in Perfect Peace

We should be at peace in situations of challenge. We should learn to ignore our "emotional reflexes." They will too often prompt us to respond negatively when going through a "Soul Evolving Process."

Losing our peace destroys us mentally and physically, and this leaves us spiritually defeated!

Be at peace in your situation. Feelings come and go. We must learn to master our emotions by not allowing a temporary situation to lead us into a permanent decision. We must master our emotions; it is the only way to overcome any situation.

Isaiah 26:3 states, "You keep him in perfect peace whose mind is stayed on you, because he trusts you." Having total confidence in our God is the only way we can be at peace in the midst of the storm. 1 John 3:19-21 tells us, "And hereby we know that we are of the truth, and shall assure our hearts before him. For if our heart condemns us, God is greater than our heart, and knoweth all things. Beloved, if our heart condemns us, *then* we have confidence toward God."

We must constantly remind ourselves that we are one with the Father, and that the kingdom of God is within us. This means that the battlefield is in the mind. We have been given the tools to win at this game called "life." With this knowledge, we truly have a blessed assurance. If your heart condemns you, it is your own doing, not that of God. The God within you is all knowing, and you are made in his image and likeness. How could you be condemned?

Conviction and Condemnation

There is a difference between conviction and condemnation. *Conviction* is defined as a firm belief. It is a state of being convinced about something. *Condemnation*, on the other hand, is defined as an unfavorable or adverse judgment; to judge or pronounce to be unfit for use or service.

1 John 3:21 tells us "Beloved, if our hearts condemn us not, then have we confidence toward God." You see, we walk and talk differently when we know who we are in God. When we know who we are in God, it causes us to realize that there is no condemnation. We have boldness in who we are and *whose* we are!

If we are to attain our natural state of peace in situations and challenges, we should never see the pursuit as detrimental. I often say that every trial produces a field of diamonds.

> Never allow the situation to get the best of you. The situation should instead cause you to grow and to get stronger and deeper into the things of God.

You must realize that each trial is only a test of your strength. Do not get caught up an illusion where God has not heard your prayers, or where he is blind to your situation. Believe in the teaching that told you of Jesus! The same spirit that abides in Jesus also abides in you. He died to give you access to the Father. Hold your peace. Keep your peace by standing on the Word of God; whatsoever we ask of him we receive of him.

> Through standing on the Word of God, we cultivate our ability to be at peace.

Why give in to fear, doubt, and worry? These things only rob you of your field of diamonds.

As believers, we have access to the Word of God. 2 Timothy 3:16-17 states, "All scripture is given by inspiration of God and is profitable for doctrine, for reproof, for correction, for instruction in righteousness; that the man of God may be perfect, thoroughly finished unto all good works". We obtain wisdom, knowledge, and power through the Word of God, even in challenging situations.

The Processed Woman is Skilled at Using What She's Got to Get What She Wants

What does it matter what you think of yourself if it is not based on truth? The opinion you have of yourself is the very thing making or breaking you. The opinion you have of yourself is either bringing you greater power to face your struggles or causing you to falter and fall. Self-confidence is either your greatest friend or your greatest enemy! What you believe about yourself is reflected in the attitudes you approach the world with each day. What you truly believe about yourself shines through as you go about your daily activities. A negative attitude is brought about when you do not understand your personal power.

A positive attitude has a strong foundation built upon truth! Truth is what God says about you; it is not the opinion of others.

God is seeks full expression through you. The great "*I AM*" is in you! We are not humans trying to have a spiritual experience; we are souls living a human experience. There is nothing more powerful than an awakened soul. The possibilities of the "*I AM*" within are infinite. The God within is limitless and therefore the law of our being is limitless. Knowing as much, we may receive and enjoy the full benefits that Jesus provided, through his acts of sacrifice and love.

> When our emotions or thoughts which consists of our beliefs, faith, and knowing manifest in response to the Word of God, they have the power to influence the course of any and all events in our lives and in the world!

The degree to which we understand and properly use our God-given power, we will manifest that same measure of blessings and power in our lives.

We cannot demonstrate beyond the limitations we place upon ourselves.

Over a period of time our faith will increase to the point of "knowing". The more our Christ consciousness is awakened, the more we begin to recognize who we are and whose we are. As a result of that recognition, more of our desires will begin to manifest in our lives.

We have been given the power to access an abundant life. In order to live an abundant life, we must know how to get it and how to keep it.

To get what we want, we must start where we are. We must utilize what we already have and constantly apply ourselves as we work through the process toward enlightenment. Elisha asked the widow, "tell me, what hast thou in the house?" (2 Kings 4:2). The solution to her problems was found in her own home. We have the ability to unlock mysteries to solve our problems by seeking answers from God. By acknowledging and living by the truth of who we are, we gradually increase our wisdom and understanding. Ultimately, this realization will produce good results!

Psalms 139:14-17 states, "I will praise thee; for I am fearfully and wonderfully made; marvelous are thy works: and that my soul knoweth right well. My substance was not hid from thee, when I was made in secret, and curiously wrought in the lowest parts of the earth. Thine eyes did see my substance, yet being unperfect; and in thy book all my members were written, which in continuance were fashioned, when as yet there was none of them. How precious also are thy thoughts unto me, O God! how great is the sum of them!"

God formed us with everything we need to become a Processed Woman, for we were wonderfully and fearfully made.

We should strive to have a greater understanding and a clearer concept of who we are day by day. In this way, our soul will know "well." We should daily learn more of the truth and apply it to our actions. By doing so, we will be on the right path and eventually experience true freedom. By standing up and claiming our God-given birthrights, we eventually "use what we have to get what we want!" Eventually, we shall manifest our heart's desires. We must simply persevere and refuse to give up.

It is a wonderful thing to know who you really are. Job 22:28 states, "Thou shalt also decree a thing, and it shall be established unto thee: and the light shall shine upon thy ways." Remember, it is not so much what you think or what you affirm, it is who is doing the thinking and affirming! Prepare to sacrifice everything to use what you have. Prepare to sacrifice everything to evolve into the vessel of God you were created to be on earth. In turn, you will receive everything!

> It is truly awesome to make conscious use of your God-given power-to feel and know that if you desire and decree a thing, it shall be established unto you.

The Processed Woman Desires to Live a Life of Integrity

Integrity

Integrity is defined as the quality of being honest and having strong moral principles. It is important to follow the laws of God in a world where everybody acts in ways far outside the sanctioned ways of God. It's a world in which everybody tries to "shine" in one way or another. The desire for power can be overwhelming unless you walk in integrity. I often remind myself that good-looking things are not always good for me!

Having moral principles has more to do with following the laws and expectations of God, rather than of humankind. This is not to say we should not follow the laws of the land in which we live. To do anything else would be foolish and cause you must pain and trouble. The laws of God maintain honesty in *all* we do. Having an upright moral character has nothing to do with your performance when others are around; to be morally correct, you must follow these same principles when no one is around. It is so easy to succumb to temptation if we have not learned from our experiences.

> Life challenges each of us to grow and mature, warning us from continuing down the same path.

The consequences of poor choices help us perfect the character within us.

We have no one to blame but ourselves if we choose to live a life beneath God's vision.

Strong moral character is built over time, but it is also developed by learning about one's true self. When you know that you are royalty, you do not act or conduct yourself like a peasant: you walk, talk, and act like the queen you are. This continues to hold true when it comes to our behavior and attitudes. We should strive daily to live righteous lives-lives others would want to emulate. The lifestyle of a Processed Woman should not bring shame upon herself or those who look up to her. Many people suffer today because they have lost confidence in those who fail to follow the same moral principles they themselves teach.

I stated earlier that *integrity* means strong moral principles. This means you are firm in your beliefs and you are not easily moved from them. Walking in integrity may cause you to lose some associates along the way, but it is much better to stand with God and have peace of mind, than to try to please someone else! It is not up to others to remember who you are. That is your job!

Have integrity in all that you do and the favor of God will follow you. You will find that good will come to you when you do good to others. You will find the love and kindness of others once love and kindness grace all of your actions. So teaches 1 Thessalonians 5:21-22: "Prove all things; hold fast to that which is good. Abstain from all appearance of evil."

Everything you do, do as unto the Lord, knowing that your reward will come from God. Always remember,

> Always remember: to see yourself only through the eyes of others can be detrimental to your mental and spiritual health!

The Processed Woman Knows She Must Overcome the Fear of Failure

Psalm 121 makes it very clear that our help comes from the Lord:

> I will lift up mine eyes unto the hills, from whence cometh my help. My help cometh from the Lord which made heaven and earth. He will not suffer thy foot to be moved: he that keepeth thee will not slumber. Behold, he that keepeth Israel shall neither slumber nor sleep. The Lord is thy keeper: the Lord is thy shade upon thy right hand. The sun shall not smite thee by day, nor the moon by night. The Lord shall preserve thee from all evil: he shall preserve thy soul. The Lord shall preserve thy going out and thy coming

in from this time forth, and even for evermore (Psalm 121:1-8).

Help does not come from people or things outside of us, but from God! Everything we will ever need in order to overcome any challenge is already in us. Paul also makes this very clear to Timothy:

> Wherefore I put thee in remembrance that thou stir up the gift of God, which is in thee by the putting on of my hands. For God hath not given us the spirit of fear; but of power, and of love, and of a sound mind (2 Timothy 1: 6-7).

Here, Paul explains to Timothy that the gift of God or power of God is already in us. But it must be stirred up, activated or acknowledged first.

The power of God cannot be effectively used in our lives when we live a life full of fear.

In this same chapter we see that the spirit of fear is put in direct opposition with the spirit of *power, love, and a sound mind.*

Fear

So what is fear? I sometimes call it *False Evidence Appearing Real*. Fear is defined as an emotion induced by a *"perceived"* threat. It is the thought that we need something or will lose something seemingly important to us.

> Fear is a problem because it affects all of our responses and decisions.

Everything we experience is coming from one or two places. The first is from the spirit of fear, which is not of God. The second is from the spirit of love, which is God!

There are two things you must do to overcome the fear of failure.

1) You must take the time to look at your fears; you have to face them instead of running from them. You must analyze them and discover what you are really afraid of. Remember, God has not given you the spirit of fear!
2) Discover what impact your fears are have on your choices, decisions, and ability to go forward and fulfill your destiny. This might include starting a new business, finding a new job, going back to school, forming a new relationship, or another desire.

When fear comes upon you, ask yourself what you think you need or might lose. Is it power, money, security, health or a relationship? Remember: God has not given you the spirit of fear!

The Bible clearly tells us that God gave us power, love, and a sound mind. A *sound mind* is a mind with an understanding of one's actions and with "reasonable knowledge" of one's family, possessions, and surroundings. Let's break this down.

1) Understanding one's actions and having "reasonable knowledge" refers to a stirring up of the gift and anointing in you.
2) "One's family" refers to an understanding of your birthright.
3) "Possessions" refers to the power you possess.
4) "Surroundings" refers to an ability to see with your spiritual eyes and not be under an illusion.

So what is the illusion? The illusion is *failure*! It is impossible for a person who knows *who* and *whose* they are to buy into the idea of failure! You may face setbacks, but you will never fail. Your steps are ordered by God, and all things are working together for your good!

The Processed Woman knows that you can replace your fears with faith.

> The *False Evidence Appearing Real* (Fear) that once crippled you can be defeated by your knowledge of the power you possess.

Remember the lesson from 2 Peter 1:3: "His divine power has given us everything we need for life and godliness through the full knowledge of the one who called us by his own glory and excellence."

You can now face every circumstance with confidence. I once read a Chinese proverb that said fear is just excitement in need of an attitude adjustment! This is so true! From this day forth, fear will no longer have power over you. You will be ready to face the world, and you will know yourself to be equipped with all of the power you will ever need!

The Processed Woman Understands the Importance of Forgiveness

"Father, forgive them for they do not know what they are doing" are Jesus's words in Luke 23:34. They set a clear example for valuing forgiveness. Jesus was in an extreme situation at the time. He had endured great pain and humiliation. The people he was trying to convince his heavenly father to forgive had a great part in his discomfort and misery. "You just don't know how bad that person has hurt me!" we often say. We let this excuse cause us to walk with our lack of forgiveness.

> The person you cannot forgive will always have power over you in some way.

Forgiveness from God is tied to our ability to forgive others. Luke 6:37 states, "Forgive and you will be forgiven." This statement plainly shows that we must learn to forgive the offenses of others. At times it may be hard, but the Processed Woman knows that her progression is tied up in connected to her ability to forgive others. As women, we often find that we have to forgive others for betrayals, lies, acts of insensitivity, disrespect, and so much more. The Processed Woman, however, can rise above the situation and forgive those she may encounter. This leaves her open to receive forgiveness from God.

Colossians 3:13 states, "Bear with each other and forgive one another if any of you has a grievance against someone. Forgive as the Lord forgave you."

God expects us to forgive others. When we make mistakes, we seek God and ask for his forgiveness. He is faithful and will forgive and forget the offense. How can we freely receive his constant forgiveness while we are unable to forgive others for more minor offenses?

Once a group of people brought a woman before Jesus, explaining that she had been caught in the act of adultery. They wanted Jesus to let them stone this woman; this is what the law required at that time in history. Jesus did something very radical. He asked that the first stone be cast by the person in the crowd who was without sin. No one in that crowd or in our world today could rightfully throw that stone.

We find it easy to see the imperfections and indiscretions of others while forgetting that God has forgiven us and set us on the right path.

The Processed Woman recognizes that she is dealing with imperfect people. She knows there are times when the people she encounters may offend, betray or act unkindly toward her. However, there are four things that the Processed Woman must do:
1) **Acknowledge**. You must be honest about how you feel about the situation. Be real with yourself and the person who has hurt you. Most importantly, be real with God! Denying your feelings will never help you heal.
2) **Forgive**. You may not forget the offense, but you must be willing to forgive. Never allow anyone or anything to keep you in "bitterness alley." It is a dark and lonely ally and it leads nowhere fast. From bitterness springs all manner of evil.
3) **Release**. Do not hold on to things. What you hold on to will eventually have a hold on you! Take charge! Do not allow yourself to be an emotional rag doll, to be tossed here and there.
4) **Move on**. You cannot walk forward while looking backward. If you try to do so, you will likely to bump into something and injure yourself. That is exactly what happens when

we refuse to move on: we hurt ourselves not the other person.

The Processed Woman knows that true forgiveness is a secret weapon to propel her forward toward her destiny. Sometimes forgiving just seems too hard to do. Perhaps the pain of the incident is just too great. In these moments, it comes down to a question: Do we choose to remain in that pain or do we choose to get up and move toward our purpose? The Processed Woman knows that it is a waste of time to throw a pity party or plot revenge.

The Processed Woman simply applies her energies to the task of moving forward. She learns from her past and moves on. Nothing good can be produced from dwelling in pain, anger and frustration. The Processed Woman recognizes that each setback is part of her journey. She learns the lesson she is meant to learn and moves on.

Sometimes forgiveness can start with forgiving ourselves. Yes, we must forgive ourselves in order to allow certain things to take place in our lives.

After forgiving ourselves, we are able to forgive others.

Healing is a process that requires daily commitment.

When you feel old feelings of hurt rise up each day, simply exercise your personal power by saying aloud "I forgive that offense." Take the energy you would spend dwelling on that past incident and direct it upon an action that will move you forward spiritually, mentally, and emotionally.

One day you will look back and realize that the mountain you once had to climb is now nothing more than a memory. It's true that although we may forgive, we do not forget. Still, the day will come when you think about that situation and find the pain gone.

The memory will no longer have an emotional sting!

I often say that only God can take a broken heart and perform a surgery so precise it does not leave a scar! You may not be able to pinpoint exactly when you forgave the person that brought chaos to your doorstep. But you actually closed the door on all of it by forgiving. Because of this action, you are so much further along on your journey to become the Processed Woman.

The Processed Woman Walks in Her Destiny and Fulfills Her Purpose

God had a purpose for you before he placed you in your mother's womb. Many times we needlessly fret because we don't believe we know about our true purpose in life. No matter what parents, friends, and relatives may say, only God can reveal this information to us.

> We must listen to our spirits and determine what God has specifically designed for us.

If a dream or goal fails to leave your mind, no matter how much time passes, that may well be your ultimate hint. Perhaps it is something you wish you could do, but life, finances, and other situations seem to always get in your way.

Have you ever felt that something awesome is going to happen, and you felt this so strongly that you know it to be true? It is beyond wishful thinking; it is something you sense will come to pass. In spite of the feeling, however, there is an enormous amount of doubt creeping up. There is also no physical evidence that your dreams could manifest into reality.

In these moments, remember the story of Abraham and Sarah. They were told they would have a son. In reality, they were old. Sarah felt she was past child-bearing age, yet she believed that she would have a son. She believed the promise, but she lacked the faith to wait for God to bring it about. Instead of waiting for it to happen, Sarah thought she would take things into her own hands and help the plan along. She acted on human knowledge and common sense. The problem is that when we intervene in God's plans, we often can delay the blessing by trying to rush it along.

It is sometimes difficult to discern whether your next step is based on God's plan for you or something you've personally dreamed up as a logical next step. True, we're not to sit back and watch things happen: there are instructions to be followed. The trick is to wait until you know deep within your spirit that the step in question is one that you must take.

Sarah delivered a healthy baby boy far past child-bearing age, even in spite of her dabbling with her purpose. God is not surprised when we make a wrong decision. He is not rattled and worried that his plan won't work; he knows that eventually his perfect plan will unfold.

Many times people give up on their purpose because they feel it is too difficult or that they lack the skills and wisdom to complete what God has told them to do. We have to recognize that God often assigns tasks that require both his help and the help of others.

> People expect a "ready-made" purpose, but most of the time we have to work our way into our purpose by preparation.

We have to determine what it would take to get from "point A" to "point B" of our purpose. After prayerful consideration, we must put a plan in place to accomplish what God has sent us here to do. Sometimes it may mean returning to college to update or obtain new skills; other times it may require networking with a different crowd, volunteering to get experience and a foot in the door, or many other methods. The possibilities are endless, but the important thing is to determine what is necessary to move forward and then do so.

The Processed Woman will often draw upon her experiences to fulfill her purpose. She must maintain a positive attitude; often times the journey is full of obstacles. The Processed Woman must remember that she must continually keep her eyes on the goal in order to avoid being derailed by distractions. Bishop T.D. Jakes once quipped, "Don't drive off of the road swatting at gnats." It is a profound statement indeed when we recognize that gnats are annoying and bothersome, much like our obstacles and distractions. Small disturbances are merely "gnats" we encounter as we make our way.

We sometimes wish we could avoid confrontations, obstacles and difficulties by hoping that the problem will just go away. This, however, only serves to make the issue worse. As a Processed Woman we must know that we are overcomeers. Part of the process is going *through* the temporary discomfort of this roadblock. Sometimes you just have to endure the pain and discomfort, knowing that it is only for an appointed time. You will emerge on the other side that much closer to your purpose.

It is during these times of troubles that we must remember to rule over our emotions. The Processed Woman recognizes the signals that may cause her emotions to go into overload, and she effectively reacts to the situation. So many times mistakes or derailments in our lives are made because of decisions based on fleeting. Always remember to never make a permanent decision based on a temporary emotion.

The Processed Woman can separate the discomfort of *now* and make a rational decision in spite of the turmoil.

The Processed Woman recognizes that if God has given her a purpose, he has definitely given her the provisions to complete it. She may have to wait for the appropriate time, but something will always come through. Perhaps she must only look at the familiar in a different way. Before giving up in frustration, the Processed Woman knows she must consider her current resources.

Above all, the Processed Woman operates with integrity. She recognizes that every short cut doesn't necessarily boast the most honest and forthcoming way to accomplish her tasks. She understands that it is more important to pay a little more or wait a little longer for the God-given opportunity or resource. As the saying goes, "All that glitters is not gold," as the saying goes; this may apply to some situations ahead of you. If it sounds too good to be true, maybe it is. That is not to say that God can't produce a profound miracle, but if it requires anything that falls outside of the Word of God, it would be safe to assume the way is not blessed. The Processed Woman knows that her reputation is far more important than saving a few dollars or time along the way.

Lastly, the Processed Woman recognizes that fulfilling her purpose is not only about her. It is always also about others. Others are hungry for the experience or encouragement that we can offer. The Processed Woman goes through her process in a way that lets her reach back and help others successfully complete their own processes. Prayer reveals the purpose, prayer reveals the path, prayer reveals and updates instructions from God, and prayer helps maintain strength as a Processed Woman pursues her journey.

One has to wonder why some people fulfill their dreams or purpose and others don't. I often think that those who see their dreams come to pass hold fast to their dream, moving ever toward it and refusing to give up. Sometimes it may even seem like hell has broken loose right before your biggest breakthrough. I am pretty sure I am not the only one who has experienced that! Nonetheless, you should still make it a habit to do at least one thing each day that will eventually move you closer to your goal.

> When you find you are growing weary from the wait, remind yourself that there is purpose in all things.

Strive to be more and do more every single day. Dig deeper, reach higher, and strive to shine brighter.

Face your fears; do not run from them.

Do not let any situation or circumstance dominate, break, or control you physically or emotionally. You are greater than any challenge you will ever face! Be encouraged and keep your head up.

No matter what the situation may be, stay motivated and encouraged. Don't you dare give up and don't you dare give in. It is all a part of the process. Embrace it. The challenges you face have not come to break you; they have come to make you into the woman God has always meant for you to be. The broken roads you travel will someday lead you to your destiny!

There is a *king in you*. Always make sure you take the jewels from every situation and never forget *your purpose is on the other side!*

www.ingramcontent.com/pod-product-compliance
Lightning Source LLC
Chambersburg PA
CBHW031420040426
42444CB00005B/659